HORRIBLE SCIENCE

ANNUAL
2010

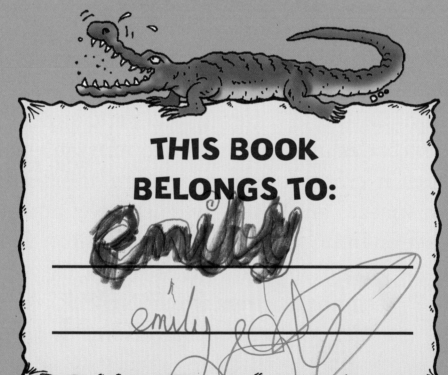

THIS BOOK
BELONGS TO:

emily

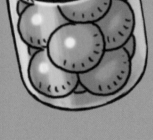

SCHOLASTIC

DEAR READER...

Welcome to your
HORRIBLE SCIENCE ANNUAL 2010!
...and what a pus-ridden, vomit-inducing treat we
have in store for you. This year's annual is
teeming with foul festering facts and super-slick
science. Get up-close and uncomfortable with
snakes 'n' crocs, soaring spacemen, the diseases
in sneezes and a beastly black hole, not to
mention brain-bending puzzles and fun-filled
things to do. It's the kind of stuff that your
science teachers would NEVER
let you get your hands on!

CONTENTS

GREEDY 'GATOR

Welcome to the marshy swamplands of Florida, USA, and take a look inside one of its biggest inhabitants, a massive female American alligator!

1. These jaws are among the strongest in the world – they can press down with a weight of up to 400 kilograms per square centimetre! But all the power is in the closing. The muscles to open the jaws are quite weak, which is why zoo-keepers can keep them shut with an elastic band.

2. If you look down the throat of a 'gator you will see it has a big flap called the palatal valve which closes to stop it swallowing too much water when opening the jaws to catch submerged prey.

3. The nostrils also have flaps to stop water going up the nose, and the ears (**3a**) also have a similar closing mechanism.

4. The eye has a third transparent eyelid to stop water getting into the eyeball. 'Gators have great night vision and a fantastic view of rapid movement. They move snappily!

5. 'Gators eat every 3–4 days, and in between digestive juices break down the fresh fodder.

6. These claws are sharp and strong – great for building nests, and also 'gator holes for the winter.

7. This leafy, woody nest is filled with hatching eggs. Babies use a special tooth (**7a**) to crack the egg open from the inside. Other young must watch out for hungry fish (**7b**), racoons (**7c**) or snapping turtles (**7d**)!

8. The scales are incredibly tough, strengthened with grains of bone called osteoderms. Armour plates called scutes protect the softer insides.

9. Males make a low bellowing mating call. Sadly this critter (**9a**) hasn't heard it!

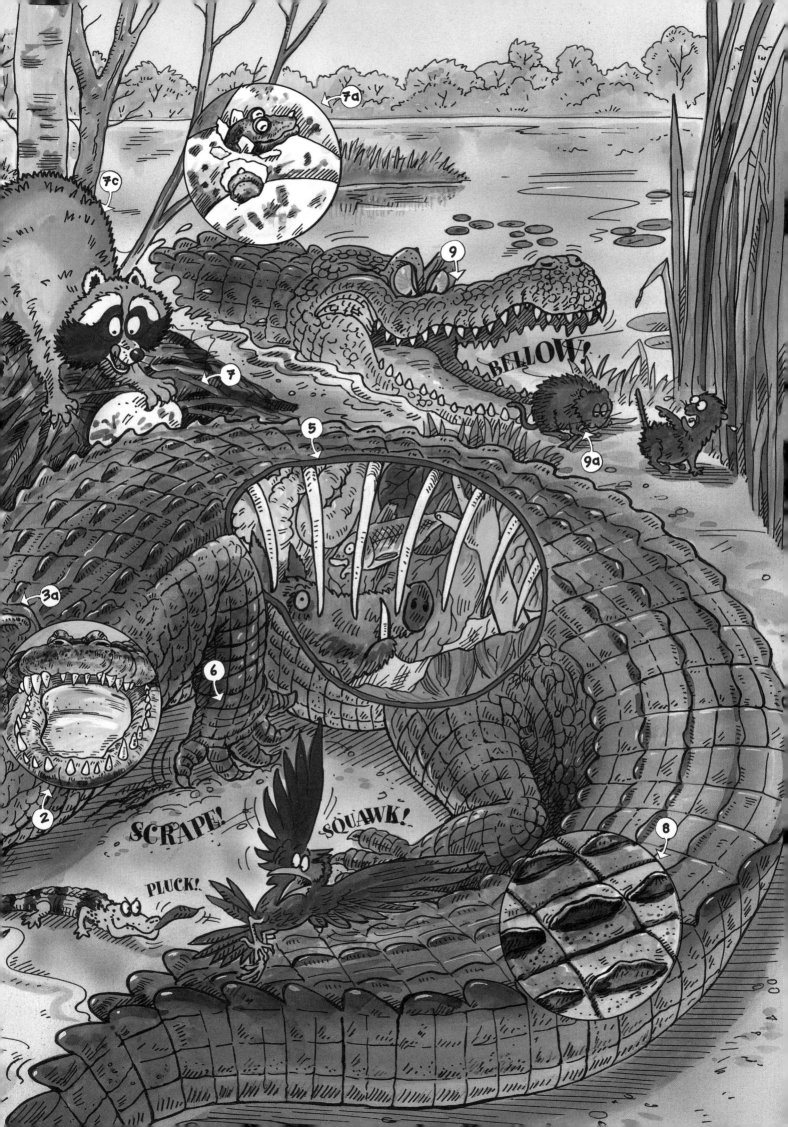

A NIGHT ON THE REPTILES

Meet Lee Ping, a locust with the lowdown on lizards – not to mention snakes, crocs and tortoises. Reptiles are the scaliest, scariest and sometimes strangest animals you could never wish to meet – and Lee should know...

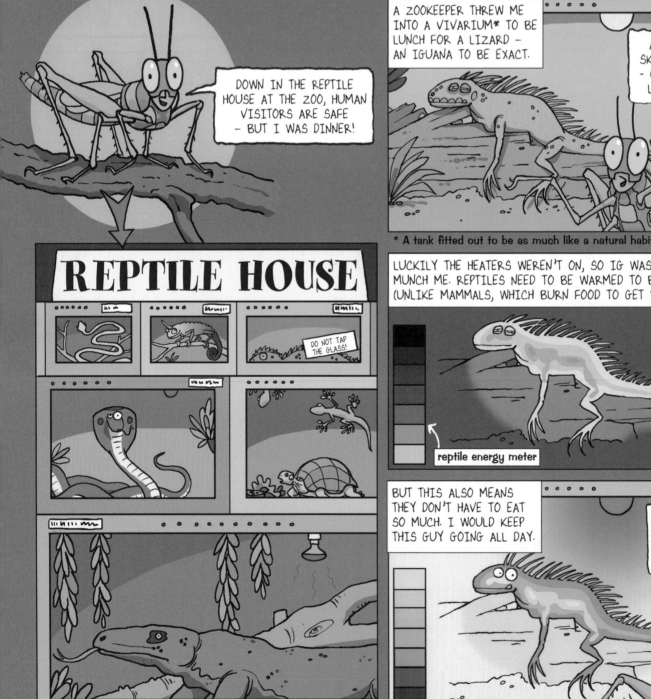

DOWN IN THE REPTILE HOUSE AT THE ZOO, HUMAN VISITORS ARE SAFE – BUT I WAS DINNER!

REPTILE HOUSE

DO NOT TAP THE GLASS!

A ZOOKEEPER THREW ME INTO A VIVARIUM* TO BE LUNCH FOR A LIZARD – AN IGUANA TO BE EXACT.

ALL REPTILES HAVE SKIN MADE OF SCALES – OVERLAPPING PLATES LIKE MINI-ARMOUR

* A tank fitted out to be as much like a natural habitat as possible.

LUCKILY THE HEATERS WEREN'T ON, SO IG WAS TOO DOZY TO MUNCH ME. REPTILES NEED TO BE WARMED TO BE ACTIVE, SEE. (UNLIKE MAMMALS, WHICH BURN FOOD TO GET WARMTH WITHIN.)

reptile energy meter

BUT THIS ALSO MEANS THEY DON'T HAVE TO EAT SO MUCH. I WOULD KEEP THIS GUY GOING ALL DAY.

OH OH – HE'S WARMING UP, WHICH IS MY CUE TO HOP IT!

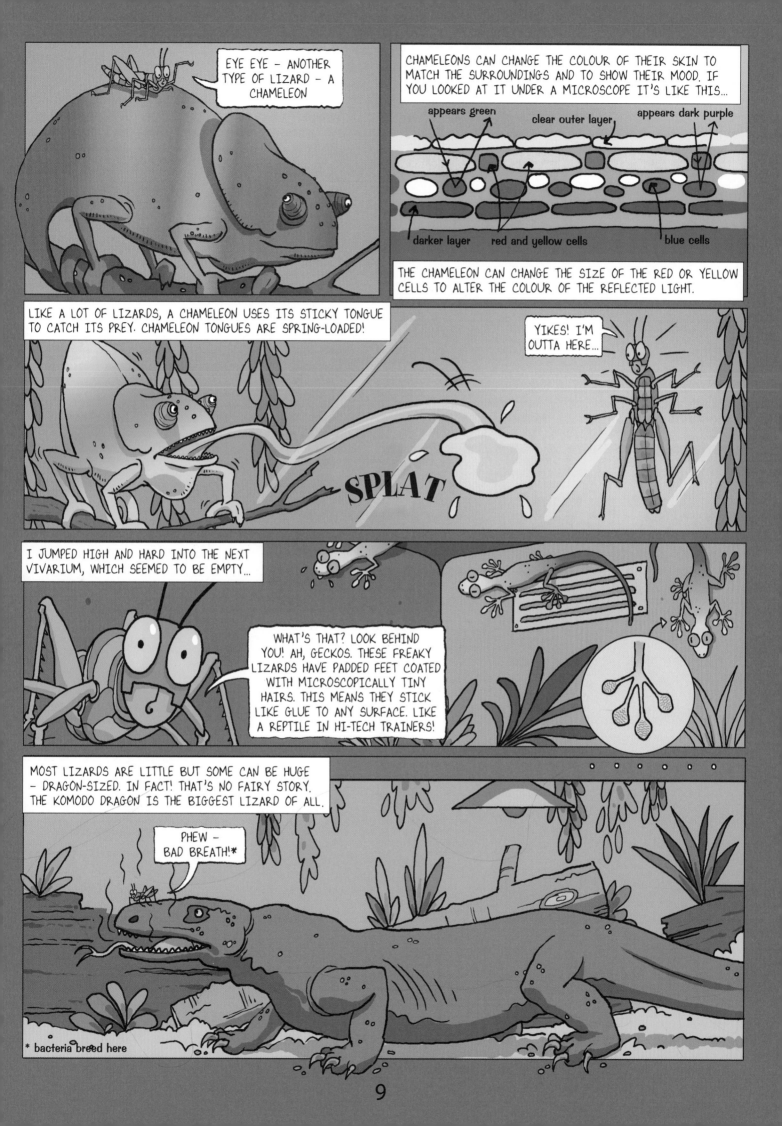

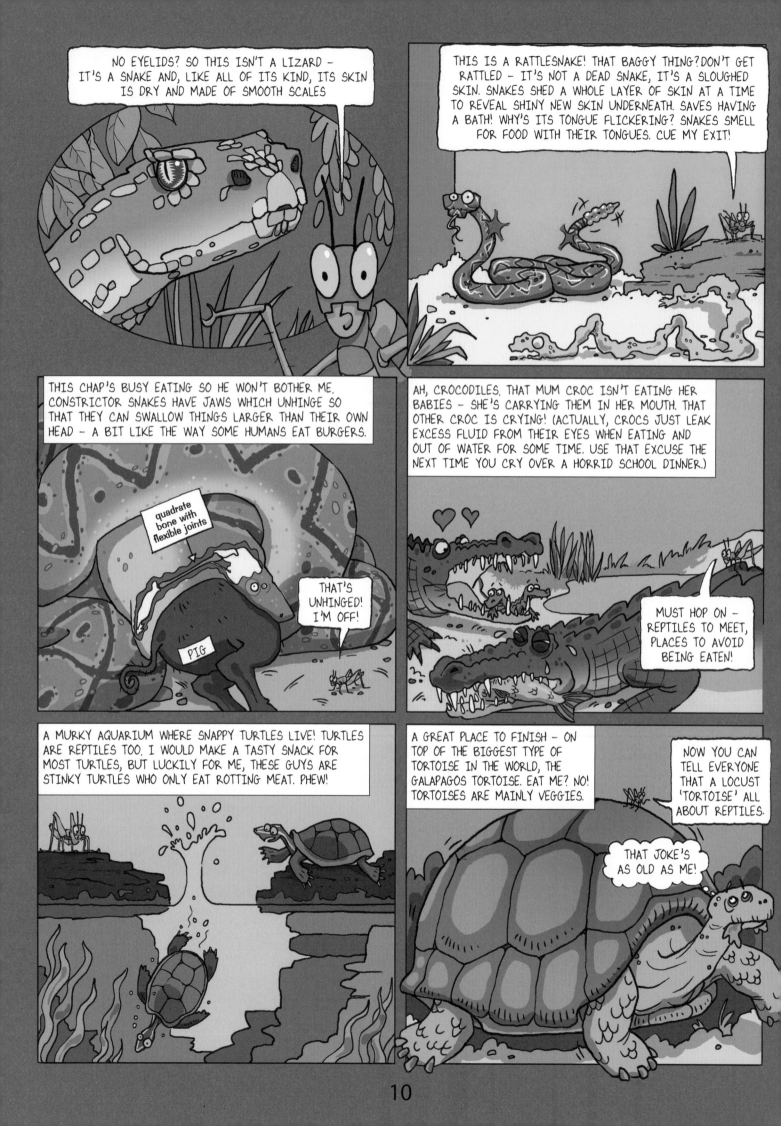

STARTLING SNAKE FACTS

Ye Olde Snake-Bite Remedies

WARNING: Almost all these remedies are about as useful as a chocolate hot-water bottle.

1. A popular remedy among US soldiers in the 1860s was to drink 4.5 litres of whiskey. (It was also popular with soldiers who hadn't been bitten!) Rating: Useless, and possibly harmful, as the combined effects of the poison and whiskey were likely to kill off any victim whatever.

THREE MORE PINTS AND YOU'LL BE AS FIT AS A FIDDLE

2. A traditional cowboy cure was to cut off your snake-bitten finger with a knife. Or you could shoot it off with your trusty six-shooter. Rating: A painful waste of time as the poison would have spread to the rest of the body before even pulling the trigger.

3. Another olde remedy, often shown in cowboy films, was to cut open the wound and ask a good friend to suck out the poison. Rating: Useless and dangerous because you could poison your friend too.

4. Hold your nose, shut tour eyes and eat a live snake. Rating: Useless and cruel – snakes have feelings too!

TREMBLE!

5. Or you could soak the bitten hand in paraffin. Rating: Smelly and useless. Oh, and don't strike a match to light your dying cigarette either!

6. How about wrapping chicken meat around the bite, then burning the meat? Rating: Utterly useless – especially for the chicken!

7. Try a toad: Romans came up with the rather rotten idea of squashing it and squeezing its juices over the wound. Rating: Cruel and useless.

8. Lastly, before you get bitten, chew some of the snake's poison glands. Or you could make a small wound in your skin and rub in a mixture of spit and poison gland. Rating: Amazingly, these may work! The Kung, San and Zulu peoples of southern Africa use these remedies. Anyone for a free trial?

Startling Snakes

NAME: King cobra
DESCRIPTION: Up to 5.5m long.
LIVES: India, southern China, South-east Asia.
FIERCE FEATURES: Has a sinister pattern of two eyes and a nose on the hood behind its head. It displays this when it's angry or scared.

HORRIBLE HABITS: Eats other snakes. (Come to think of it, this habit could be quite useful.)
THE BAD NEWS: Its venom is strong enough to kill an elephant. So we humans don't stand a chance.

NAME: Okinawa habu

DESCRIPTION: Up to 2m long. Slender body; blotchy yellow ringed markings.
LIVES: Okinawa and nearby islands, Pacific Ocean.
FIERCE FEATURES: Heat-detectors on this pit viper's head help it to find warm living flesh.
HORRIBLE HABITS: Enjoys snaking into houses through tiny crevices.
THE BAD NEWS: Enjoys biting people.
VERY BAD NEWS: Its venom is deadly poisonous.

NAME: Black mamba
DESCRIPTION: 2–3.5m long. It's the largest poisonous snake in Africa.
LIVES: Africa – south of the Sahara Desert.
FIERCE FEATURES: This slippery customer is said to move as fast as a galloping horse.

HORRIBLE HABITS: It can swallow a whole rat, from snout to tail and digest it in just 9 hours. Most snakes take more than 24 hours. Just two drops of its venom can make a human drop down dead.

RAMPANT REPTILES

Welcome to the awesome Amazon jungle, full of hungry life that'll snap up anything if it's edible! From scales to tails, claws to jaws, it's where reptiles rule the roost!

SQUEEZE

SPLASH!

SPLASH!

1. This giant anaconda, the bulkiest reptile, must dislocate its jaws to swallow a dead antelope whole!

2. Meanwhile another anaconda will sick up a half-digested feed because it feels the temperature isn't right to digest it.

3. An emerald boa is a constrictor, squeezing its prey until they are dead. Meanwhile a rainbow boa's **(3a)** colourful markings give it away.

4. A black iguana is an expert fly catcher – its lightning-quick tongue is super-sticky!

5. The matamata is cousin to the turtle **(5a)**. It has a flat head, unusual scutes (scale plates), and a flexible snout.

6. Meanwhile, a yellow-spotted sideneck turtle walks slowly on land, eating leaves and grass. It also chomps on small fish and worms.

7. The turnip-tail gecko's grey-brown markings are great for camouflage, and it makes a high-pitched chirping as a mating call.

8. This spectacled caiman, is cold-blooded like all reptiles and must bask in the sunshine to heat up its blood until warm enough to move.

9. This common caiman is warmed up, and is enjoying a fish breakfast.

10. Waiting until his larger cousin has eaten, this small caiman is hanging about for leftovers.

11. The anole lizard has a brightly coloured chest for showing off to the female. What a poser!

12. This Amazon egg-eater snake is stretching its jaws around an egg.

13. This Amazon racerunner lizard is escaping the jaws of a hungry crocodile. It's one of the fastest reptiles, running at 29km/h!

14. The common glossy racer snake isn't as fast, but sure is quick enough to catch a worm!

15. Another fan of slow-moving prey is the banded snail-sucker. Look out for stripy markings, you snails!

SCALY MONSTERS

With nearly 8000 species, reptiles have been on this planet for about 300 million years – far longer than mammals or birds. So let's get to grips with what makes a reptile, and make it 'snappy'!

Rampant reptiles have spread out and adapted to environments all over the world, except the poles as they're not keen on cold climates. This is because they're what herpetologists (reptile and amphibian boffins) call ectotherms (say ek-toe-therms), which means they need an outside heat source, such as sunshine, to heat their blood to the right temperature so they can stay active. So, reptiles spend their whole lives moving between sun and shade. But what else do they do?

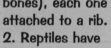

REVOLTING REPTILES FACT FILE

NAME: Reptiles
BASIC FACTS:

1. Reptiles are vertebrates (they have backbones). Snakes have 100 to 300 vertebrae (back bones), each one attached to a rib.

2. Reptiles have lungs and breathe air, even the ones that slither around in water.

3. All reptiles are cold-blooded – they can't heat themselves from the inside.

4. Crocs, alligators, turtles and tortoises and some lizards have special, bony armour-like scales.

5. Most reptiles lay soft-shelled eggs, but a few, like anacondas and British common lizards, give birth to live young (they are viviparous).

6. Legged reptiles have a sprawling gait, with limbs sticking out at the side. Crocs can turn their feet inwards and walk with them under their bodies.

KILLER FACTS: Some reptiles are poisonous – killing their prey with venom. Mostly, the viciously venomous reptiles are snakes but there are a couple of lizards too: beaded lizards and Gila monsters which can give a poisonous bite.

Leaping lizards

The largest reptile group is the lizards with more than 4500 different species spread farther afield than all the other reptile families. They thrive in warm climates, especially deserts, as the sunshine suits them and they can survive on less food than warm-blooded animals. Lizards are mostly four-legged, but some have only two legs and others, such as slow-worms, are completely legless and are often mistaken for snakes. All lizards are scaly and some have horny frills or sharp spikes to protect them from predators.

Snappy snakes

The next largest reptile family (after lizards) is the s-s-s-snakes! There are about 2900 species around the world – all related by their lack of visible legs, no hearing and unmoveable eyelids.

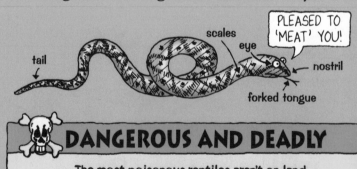

☠ DANGEROUS AND DEADLY

The most poisonous reptiles aren't on land – they're in the seas around India and east Asia. Sea-snake poison is dozens of times more deadly than any other snake poison. That's the bad news. The good news is that sea snakes don't enjoy biting humans. So, Indian fishermen often pull the suckers from their nets using their bare hands! Brave...?

OR JUST PLAIN STUPID!

Reptile scales

- The heaviest reptile is the saltwater crocodile, weighing up to 1000kg.
- The smallest reptile is the dwarf gecko, which measures only 17mm and could fit on the end of your finger.
- The longest reptile is the reticulated python, which grows to 10 metres.
- Tortoises are the longest living reptiles: reaching a ripe old age of 150 years.
- The world's fastest reptile on land is the spiny-tailed iguana of Costa Rica. It has been clocked at 35km/h!

Crafty crocs

The crocodilian family includes 23 different species of crocodiles, alligators, caimans and gharials. Many boffins believe they're the last survivors of a reptile branch that produced the dinosaurs and birds. They've been around for over 200 million years and, as perfectly designed killers, they've remained top of the food chain in the rivers and swamps that they live in.

I FEEL A REAL OLD CROCK

Reptile in a box

Turtles and tortoises are another ancient reptilian family. The 300 or so species have one common feature – they have an outer protective shell of about 60 horny plates (called scutes) as part of their skeleton. The creature inside can't crawl out because its shell is attached to its spine and rib cage. The shell's top is called the carapace and the bottom is the plastron.

Living fossil

The smallest family of reptiles has only one member: the rare tuatara. It looks like a lizard, but is far more primitive – it has a strong skull, and in the middle of its forehead there's a spot-like third 'pineal eye', which just sees light and helps regulate exposure to it.

WHAT D'YA MEAN, THREE EYES?

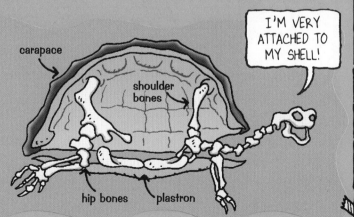

carapace

shoulder bones

hip bones   plastron

I'M VERY ATTACHED TO MY SHELL!

Bet you never knew!

Most reptiles lay soft, leathery eggs, and then call it a day – they don't stick around to protect the eggs from harm, or keep them warm. But a few reptile mothers do, and care for their babies in other ways:

1. The tokay gecko's soft eggs harden in the dry air and stick to the surface they're laid on.

2. The Nile monitor lizard lays eggs in termite mounds. The heat from the termites helps to incubate the eggs.

3. Before settling down for a seven-month pregnancy, the female giant green anaconda of South America has a last feast – her male mate!

WHAT SHALL WE DO? IT'S OUR LAST NIGHT!

COME OVER FOR DINNER!

4. Most crocodilian mothers guard their nests and protect their young for up to a year, even carrying babies in their mouths when danger approaches.

5. Komodo dragon parents hang around the nest during hatching time – not to help, but to eat babies!

MMM, JELLY BABIES!

HOW SWEET

HOW TO CLING LIKE A GECKO

There's a weird lounge lizard called a gecko that can walk up walls and across ceilings. It lives in warm climates and can give you quite a fright as it peers down at you in bed! Try this experiment to scare your reptilian relatives.

You will need:
- a small toy lizard (or modelling clay to make you own)
- Blu-Tack
- a watch or clock with a second hand
- a table

WARNING!
Don't try this on anyone who has a weak heart – the fright could be too much for them! And make sure the table isn't laid with priceless china – you don't want any expensive breakages! Blu-Tack can be messy – keep it off fabrics and delicate surfaces.

1 Find a small plastic or rubber lizard or similar looking creature. Alternatively, make one of your own using modelling clay – but it needs to look quite lifelike. Use different coloured clay to make some scary ugly spots!

2 Take four small blobs of Blu-Tack and stick them to the undersides of the gecko's feet. You'll need to experiment with different sized blobs later on, so the size of the first ones isn't too important.

3 Stick the gecko to the underside of a meal table and use a watch to time how long it takes to fall down.

4 Adjust the size of the blobs of Blu-Tack until the gecko can stay stuck up for several minutes before falling down.

5 Just before a mealtime, stick the gecko under the table where your soppy sister or dozy aunt, for example, will be sitting. Hopefully it will fall on someone's foot, or into their lap, just when they've bitten into an oozing cream cake. EEEEKKK!

PUZZLES

SPOT THE DIFFERENCE

There are six differences between these two scenes – see if you can spot them.

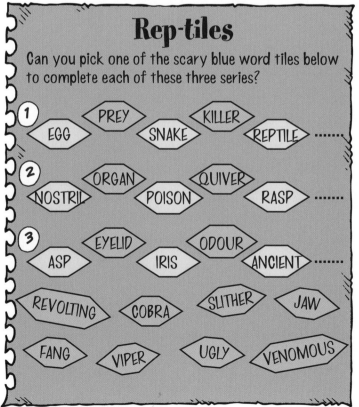

Lazy Lizard Race

One sunny afternoon, two lazy lizards enter a race. The most sluggish lizard is given a one-hour head start to complete the distance, which is 80 metres. He crawls at a lazy speed of just 20 metres per hour. The fitter lizard travels a bit faster, at 30 metres per hour, but he starts an hour later. Which lizard will be nearer the finish when they meet alongside, and how many kilometres nearer?

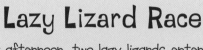

Crazy Camouflage

The joker has shed a sliver of his skin of many colours. Can you find the correct piece to fill the pattern?

WHICH REPTILE DID DOROTHY MEET IN THE DESERT? … THE LIZARD OF OZ! BOOM, BOOM!

HE'S A STAND-UP CHAMELEON!

1 2 3 4

Rep-tiles

Can you pick one of the scary blue word tiles below to complete each of these three series?

1 EGG PREY SNAKE KILLER REPTILE ....

2 NOSTRIL ORGAN POISON QUIVER RASP ....

3 ASP EYELID IRIS ODOUR ANCIENT ....

REVOLTING COBRA SLITHER JAW

FANG VIPER UGLY VENOMOUS

17

GIVE ME SPACE!

Space station living is cramped and a bit crazy. You must eat foul food, strap yourself down, and the toilet is terribly weird! See how our astronauts survive their awesome, often awful space life, and hear the horrors it does to your health!

1. Floating through space, the station often turns upside down, so the floor, wall and ceiling have to be painted different colours so you can tell which is which!

2. Because of zero gravity, you must strap yourself down when sleeping. It's not too comfortable and it's good to wear eyeshades because the Sun rises and sets every hour – very disturbing!

3. Washing is a serious business in space. Wet shaving is a must because a dry shave means little hairs will float everywhere. Showers (**3a**) are taken inside plastic bags, otherwise the water gets into all the instruments!

4. With limited space and less effort to move, exercise is very important as muscles can waste away. But astronauts beware! Zero gravity causes your blood to linger higher up in the body, especially your head, so you might get a red and swollen face!

5. When using the space toilet you must be strapped in so your bum and the seat are sealed together. This is because the toilet bowl works in a vacuum, sucking out your waste (**5a**)! Your poo and pee are dumped into space later.

6. Space food is really horrible! It's mostly dried and anything crumbly is covered in gelatin to stop the crumbs floating about.

7. If you're on a space walk, get tethered or you'll float far away!

8. Watch out! Even small space debris travelling at high speed can be very dangerous, passing straight through the ship or causing explosions.

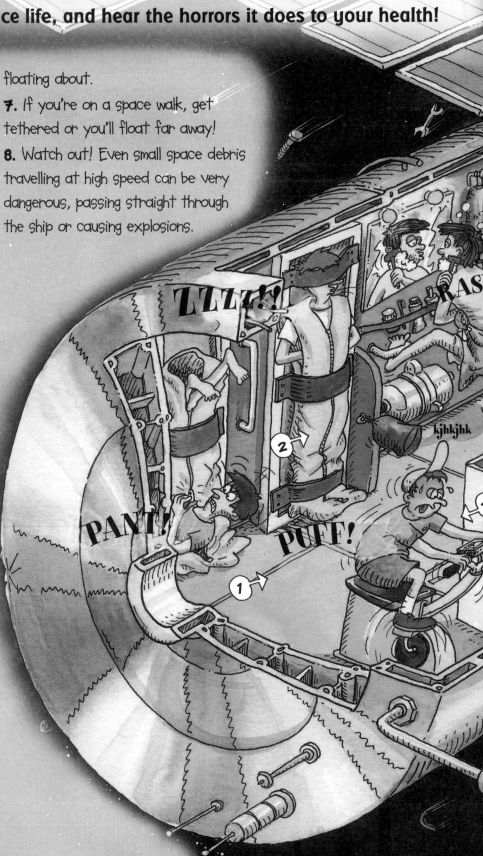

RACE FOR THE STARS

This is the story of two sometimes nutty nations – the USA and the USSR (Russia) – who hated each other's guts, and how neither wanted to lose face in a silly space race...

IT'S 1945. WORLD WAR II ENDS AND SOON TWO FORMER ALLIES FIND THEMSELVES IN A DEADLY 'ARMS RACE'...

USA

USSR*

... BUT THIS WAS ALSO ABOUT TO BECOME A SPACE RACE.

American missiles

Russian missiles

RUSHING TO BUILD THE MOST BOMBS AND MISSILES, BOTH SIDES GO AFTER THE BEST ROCKET SCIENTISTS IN THE WORLD, MOST OF WHOM ARE GERMAN.

* countries ruled by Russia

THE USA GRAB EX-NAZI ROCKET WHIZZ WERNHER VON BRAUN.

WERNER VON BRAUN

'K'

?

IN 1957 THE USSR NIPPED AHEAD WITH THE FIRST EVER SATELLITE INTO SPACE – SPUTNIK 1.

DARN THOSE PESKY RUSKIES!

1ST SATELLITE

THE WASHINGTON POST

FIRST EVER SATELLITE! SPUTNIK 1

4 Oct 1957

THE RUSSIANS NAB A TEAM OF GERMAN SCIENTISTS TO WORK WITH THEIR MYSTERIOUS TOP ROCKET MAN. THE SPACE RACE HAD BEGUN...

21

AWFUL ORBIT

Outer space is just 100km away. If you could drive there it'd only take you an hour. But it's a mean and fearfully frightening place where some really far out things happen...

Just staying alive in space is terribly tricky. Without a protective spaceship or spacesuit, astronauts would die in seconds. Here's what would happen if you absent-mindedly nipped out of your spaceship...

life of its own. Drinks form floating wet little balls. Everything has to be strapped down – and that includes YOU when you sleep! Crunchy, crispy foods are OUT, and going to the toilet is just out of this world!

DEAD DISGUSTING

- There's no air in space so without a spacesuit you'd start to suffocate immediately... and because there's no air, there's no air pressure.
- All your body bits with air or fluid in them would start to expand. Your eyes, guts and liver would go pop! Your lungs would turn inside out.
- Space is cold. It gets colder than –100°C in the shade, but with no atmosphere to protect you from the Sun's rays, it gets hotter than 120°C in the sunlight. You'd frazzle like a burger on a barbie on the side facing the Sun, while your skin would freeze solid on the other side.
- The radiation blasting out from the Sun would start to cook your insides like a microwave oven, and... with no atmosphere to carry sound, no one would hear you scream...

Oh well, at least there's one bonus – with no bacteria in space, your body wouldn't rot – you'd just be freeze-dried. N-ice!

That floating feeling

In fact, life inside your space capsule can be pretty nasty. At the speed you're whizzing round Earth, the effects of gravity disappear. The result is sometimes called 'zero-gravity', but it doesn't mean there's no gravity. (If there was nothing to pull your spaceship towards Earth, it'd fly off into space!) It does mean everything in your spaceship becomes 'weightless' and takes on a

FEARSOME FALLING FACT FILE

NAME: Freefall

THE FOUL FACTS: Imagine being in a lift when suddenly the cable breaks. SNAP! The floor races away from you and your stomach lurches horribly as the lift and you plunge to certain death. But after a while you start to float. Weird! This is because the lift and everything in it have stopped accelerating and are falling at the same speed. This is freefall. It's wonderful! Then... WHAM!

THE DEATH-DEFYING DETAILS: In orbit around Earth you never crash to ground because you're hurtling around the planet at about 27,000km/h like the Space Shuttle. But it's not all plain sailing, freefall has some rather gruesome side effects...

HOT SHUTTLE SCUTTLE

The Shuttle has been used to bus astronauts and cargo to and from the International Space Station. Blast off isn't exactly a gas, but re-entry is a white-hot, white-knuckle ride.

1. With its 46m-tall Solid Rocket Boosters (SRBs) and External fuel Tank (ET), the Shuttle looks a bit like Thunderbird 2 with attitude. Two minutes after blast off the SRBs (**1a**) are ditched. After 9 minutes the ET goes (**1b**). What remains is known as the orbiter (**1c**). It looks a bit like a transporter plane, but circling Earth at about 28,000km/h, it's still F.A.B!

2. The crew spends 7–16 days cooped up in the front decks.

3. They can open and close the payload bay doors to take out or add cargo and make repairs remotely.

4. When the time comes to return to Earth, an Orbital Manoeuvring System (OMS) slows the craft, changing its orbit so it starts to fall. The crew flip the orbiter upside down (**4a**), turning its heat-resistant tiles towards the Sun, and flying it backwards

to lose speed. (Don't panic!) Next they turn right way up (**4b**), burning left-over fuel as a safety measure.

5. The orbiter hits Earth's atmosphere at an angle of about 40°. Temperatures on the nose cone and leading edges of the wings soar to 1650°C (**5a**). Fortunately, ceramic tiles protect the hottest spots (**5b**). Phew!

6. Once in the atmosphere proper, the orbiter flies in a series of S-shapes to slow it. The undercarriage comes down about 600m from the ground.

PHEW, WHAT A SCORCHER!

STAY COOL!

MUMMY!

GLOW!

BOOST

ROAR

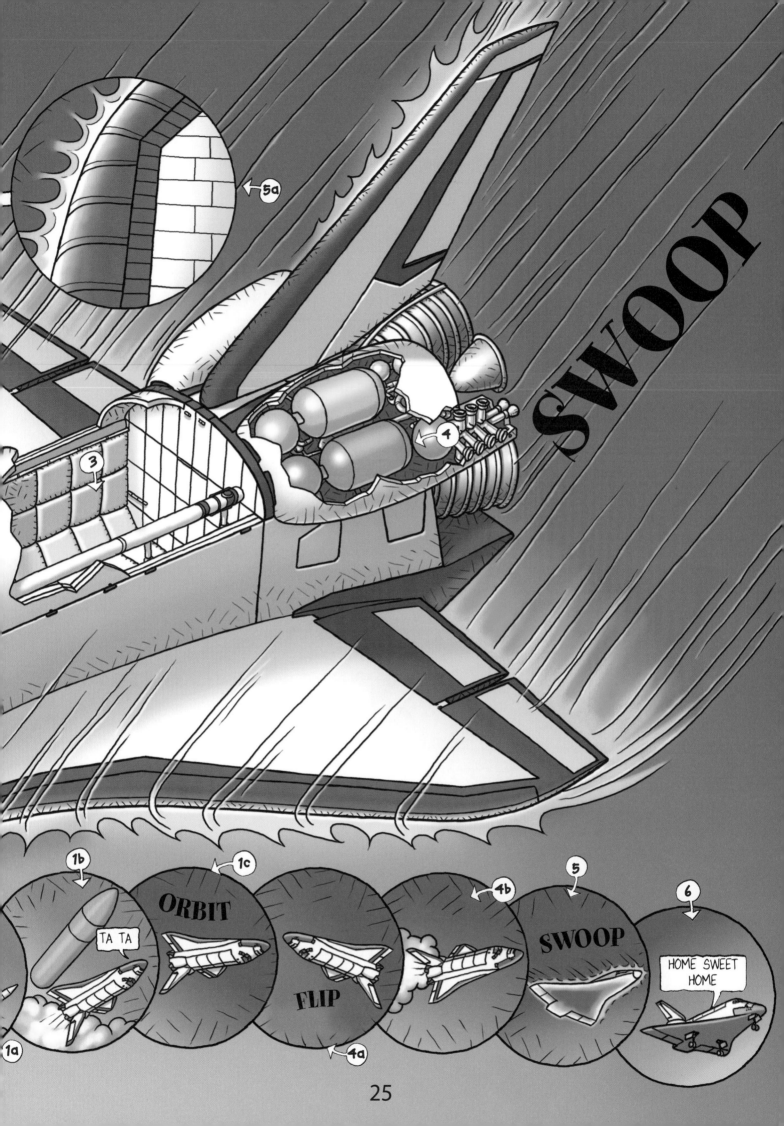

RIG UP A RASCALLY ROCKET

As you're unlikely to find a spare cylinder of rocket fuel lying about the house, here's a simple rocket you can make using the power of compressed air and a good squeeze.

You will need:
- 1-litre plastic bottle (with screw-on cap)
- a corkscrew
- two straws, one wider than the other
- Blu-Tack
- stiff paper or cardboard
- scissors
- sticky tape
- fin template

fin template

1 First make your launcher. Ask an adult to help you make a hole in the plastic bottle cap with the corkscrew.

TWIST

WARNING!
when you see this symbol, ask for help from an adult.

TEE HEE!

SQUASH!

2 Poke the straw with the smaller diameter into the hole and seal around the edges, inside and out, with two 'sausages' of Blu-Tack.

TOP TIP
Straws from fast-food restaurants are often wider than the ones you buy in the shops.

SPIN!

3 Now to make your missile! Take the wider straw and add a small blob of Blu-Tack on to one end of it. Cut out three rocket tail fins, using the template, and stick them on to the other end of the straw.

WHOOSH!

SQUEEZE

4 It's launch time! Slide the rocket on to the straw of the 'launcher'. Aim your rocket away from other people and fragile objects. Start the countdown: 5..4..3..2..1.. WE HAVE LIFT OFF! Squeeze the bottle hard and watch your rocket fly across the room.

PUZZLES

Savage Space-farers

Men and women aren't the only things on Earth to have visited space. Before the astronauts got there, dozens of different 'furry-nauts' were fired into the blue. Later on, astro-animals were used in space experiments. Can you spot the spoof space critters?

Stars In Their Eyes

Not all nations choose to call their star sailors 'astronauts'. For each of the nations shown below, see if you can pick the correct term from the following list. (But watch out — one's made up!) They are: astronaut cosmonaut spationaut taikonaut argonaut

27

SEND IN THE CLONES!

Desperate for more laughs, Clarence the ageing Clown has been creating clones of himself. But will the young clowns do what he wants?

1. Clarence is using the same method scientists used in 1996 to clone Dolly the sheep in Edinburgh, Scotland.

2. Clarence swabs a skin sample from the inside of his cheek and places it in the Petri dish (**2a**). Looking under a microscope, we see that the cell contains a nucleus (**2b**) containing all the DNA information he needs.

3. Clarence's friend Belinda the Bearded Lady has kindly donated one of her egg cells. But to avoid including information from her DNA, Clarence must remove the nucleus (**3a**) from the cell with a sharp pipette (**3b**), holding it still with a blunt pipette (**3c**).

4. Now crazy Clarence must remove his nucleus from his own cell, sucking it up with the sharp pipette (**4a**). He then transfers it into Belinda's empty egg cell (**4b**), by squirting it out again.

5. Clarence must now add a growth serum, a chemical agent that settles his nucleus inside the egg cell.

6. This takes some time but then the cells begin to divide, just like a normal fertilized egg cell.

7. The ball of cells is placed in a fantasy baby-grower. Cells continue to divide (**7a**), forming a tiny, unborn version of Clarence. Nine months later it 'hatches'.

8. Crazy Clarence's clones are genetically identical but might not want to clown at all (**8a**) and (**8b**)!

28

CODE CRACKERS

Ever wondered why you look like your parents or why you and your brother or sister look alike? Well you're not the only one! This is the terribly twisted tale of the gene geniuses who tried to unravel the secret code of life...

FOR CENTURIES THINKERS PUZZLED OVER HOW FAMILY TRAITS PASS FROM ONE GENERATION TO THE NEXT...

GREEK GEEK HIPPOCRATES RECKONED THAT YOU ARE AN AVERAGE OF BOTH YOUR PARENTS - THE WAY YOU LOOK COMES FROM MIXING MYSTERIOUS DROPLETS FROM EACH.

BUT IF THAT WAS THE CASE, A TALL MUM AND A SHORT DAD WOULD ONLY HAVE MEDIUM-SIZED OFFSPRING. IN FACT, OVER GENERATIONS, TRAITS WOULD JUST TEND TO BECOME MORE AND MORE AVERAGE AND BORING...

HIPPO'S THEORY OBVIOUSLY WASN'T QUITE RIGHT. EVEN SO, IT WASN'T DISPROVED FOR 2300 YEARS.

IN 1856, AN AUSTRIAN MONK CALLED GREGOR MENDEL STARTED BREEDING PEA PLANTS. HE CROSS-BRED TWO STRAINS, ONE WITH PURPLE FLOWERS AND ONE WITH WHITE. (IN ALL, HE CROSSED ABOUT 28,000 PLANTS.)

WHAT! PEA SOUP AGAIN, BROTHER MENDEL?

NOT FOR YOU, BRO....

THERE'S NO PEAS FOR THE WICKED!

MENDEL ~~HIPPOCRATES~~ RULES O.K

THE PEA-MEDDLING MONK'S DISCOVERIES KNOCKED HIPPO'S THEORY FOR SIX. WHEN PURPLE AND WHITE FLOWERS WERE CROSSED THEY DIDN'T RESULT IN A MUSHY MIX OF COLOURS BUT WICKED WHITE OR PURE PURPLE PLANTS. ARE WE ALL PEAS IN A POD? NO WAY!

MENDEL REALISED THAT TRAITS FROM BOTH PARENTS DON'T 'MIX', THEY 'COMBINE' IN PREDICTABLE WAYS. HE CALLED THE INHERITED BITS 'PARTICLES'. (BUT IN 1909, DANISH BOTANIST, WILHELM LUDWIG JOHANNSEN CAME UP WITH THE NAME 'GENE' - FROM THE WORD 'GENOS' MEANING 'ORIGIN' IN...)

...GREEK! YIPPEE!

THE HUNT WAS ON TO FIND THE GENE. IN 1879 GERMAN BIOLOGIST WALTHER FLEMING SPOTTED SOME STRANGE WORM-LIKE BITS WHEN HE STAINED SOME PLANT CELLS. THESE ARE CALLED 'CHROMOSOMES'.

BE OFF! I WON'T HAVE SILLY JOKES ABOUT MY HUSBAND STAINING HIS GENES!

IN 1910 THOMAS H MORGAN AND ALFRED H STURTEVANT FOUND THAT CHROMOSOMES CARRY GENETIC INFORMATION. THEY USED FRUIT FLIES - THEIR FOUR-WEEK LIFESPAN MEANS THEY GROW UP FAST AND BREED LIKE CRAZY. TROUBLE IS, THEY ALL LOOK ALIKE!

LOOK FOR THE ONE WITH WHITE EYES!

EGAD! THEY'RE BREEDING IN THEIR THOUSANDS!

HELP ME!

MEANWHILE ANOTHER FLY FANCIER AND GENETICS RESEARCHER, HERMANN JOSEPH MULLER, FOUND OUT THAT X-RAYS MADE GENES MUTATE.

BUT STILL NO ONE KNEW WHAT WAS ACTUALLY PASSING ON FAMILY TRAITS. IN 1928, FREDERICK GRIFFITH'S NASTY EXPERIMENTS (INFECTING MICE WITH PNEUMONIA VIRUSES) PROVED THAT DNA IN THE CHROMOSOME WAS DOING IT - AND IT WAS JUST HARD CHEESE FOR THE MICE!

FEELING DOWN IN THE MOUSE

HONK

LEMSQUEAK

TO CRACK THE SECRET OF THE GENE, SCIENTISTS NEEDED TO UNRAVEL DNA AND WORK OUT HOW IT FITTED TOGETHER. WHILE JAMES WATSON AND FRANCIS CRICK WERE BUILDING A MODEL IN CAMBRIDGE...

IT'S SPIRALLING OUT OF CONTROL!

IT'S GIVING ME A CRICK IN THE NECK

...TWO OTHER SCIENTISTS WERE HARD AT WORK IN LONDON.

SINGLETON MAURICE WILKINS AND LOVELY ROSALIND FRANKLIN WERE LOOKING AT THE CHEMISTRY OF DNA. BUT THERE WAS BAD CHEMISTRY BETWEEN THEM!

HUH! SHE TREATS ME AS IF I WERE HER ASSISTANT

HUH! HE TREATS ME AS IF I WERE HIS ASSISTANT!

STILL THEY SUCCEEDED AND PASSED ON THEIR RESULTS TO CRICK AND WATSON.

IN 1962, WATSON, CRICK AND WILKINS GOT NOBEL PRIZES FOR THEIR WORK (AT THE SAME TIME AS THE AUTHOR JOHN STEINBECK, WHO WROTE THE NOVEL 'OF MICE AND MEN')!

OF MICE AND MEN

HEY LOOK! SOME RECOGNITION - AT LAST!

SADLY, ROS NEVER GOT AN AWARD.

BUT THAT WAS JUST THE BEGINNING. IN 1966 THE GENETIC CODE WAS CRACKED, OPENING THE DOOR FOR GENETIC ENGINEERING AND CLONING. IT SEEMED THE SECRET OF LIFE WAS AS EASY AS ABC. READ ON TO FIND OUT MORE ABOUT THIS TWISTING TALE...

GAGA

G

A A

A C T G

C T A G

VICIOUS VARIETY

Over the ages animals can undergo some amazing alterations - it's the secret of their survival. But how do they do it? If you thought that mutants only existed in scary movies, think again...

If you look at animals closely enough, you often find that they already have the essential equipment for evolving into something new. Shrink a bit here, stretch a bit there and they can be transformed into something that looks completely different. These days boffins do it artificially by snipping and splicing genes.

But most of the differences between individual animals occur naturally. This is called 'variation' by scientists, and it's the rotten reason that no one can get rid of the mean and miserable disease malaria.

Pesky parasites

Some mosquitoes carry squirming parasites that get squirted into your veins while they are sucking your blood. These give you a fever with horribly high temperatures and can even attack your brain! Scientists have invented all kinds of drugs to kill the malarial parasites – and at first they're usually successful – but a few parasites always survive. This is because there are small differences between individual parasites. There are always a lucky few that are naturally protected

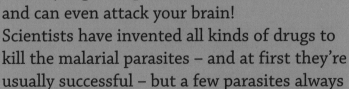

from the chemical poisons. These vile variants survive in someone's body and are passed around when another mosquito sucks their blood and then moves on to another victim. If it wasn't for the fact that these parasites are constantly changing, we might have got rid of this disgusting disease long ago. The trouble is, the malarial meanies keep evolving and stay one step ahead of the scientists.

Marvellous mutants

When characteristics of individual living things change slightly, they're called mutants. The changes are called mutations. We often think of mutations as ghastly, unnatural deformities – but sometimes mutations are useful. When animals change – when people start attacking them with chemical sprays – then the right kind of mutation can be very useful indeed.

Bet you never knew!

When polar bears first arrived in the Arctic, they had brown fur, but over time some of them mutated and began to grow white fur. Those bears that still had brown fur found it harder to sneak up on seals in the snow, so they were less able to feed themselves... and slowly died out.

ZANY ZOO

Luminous porkers, fainting goats, naked cats – all the critters here have been either selectively bred or genetically modified. Enjoy your visit!

1. Celestial goldfish look skywards, so they can't see where they're going and bubble-eyes (1a) have water sacks under the eyes.

2. All domestic dogs, from the wrinkly shar pei, mop-like komondor (2a) and pugnacious boxer (2b) to the tiny yapping chihuahua (2c) and the bloodhound (2d) are descended from one wolf-like ancestor.

3. These pigs have been genetically modified to glow in the dark.

4. Fainting goats have a mutant gene that makes them fall over when stressed. Shepherds used to use them as decoys to divert wolves from their sheep. (Bet that got their goat!)

5. Most oddities are bred simply for cuteness or as curiosities. There's tufty and frizzle chickens (5a). Then there's our mini-donkey mum, Oats, and her baby, donkey Oaty (Don Quixote – oh forget it!) (5b).

6. Eight out of ten cats prefer fur – but not the hairless sphinx who looks cool without! (There's even a nude mouse bred for labs) (6a). Don't forget the flappers...

7. ...like the trumpeter, Jacobin (7a) and Roller (7b) pigeons. But if you're thinking of buying an extreme breed as a pet, watch it. Their unusualness...

8. ...can (as with the lop-eared rabbit), be their downfall (8a)!

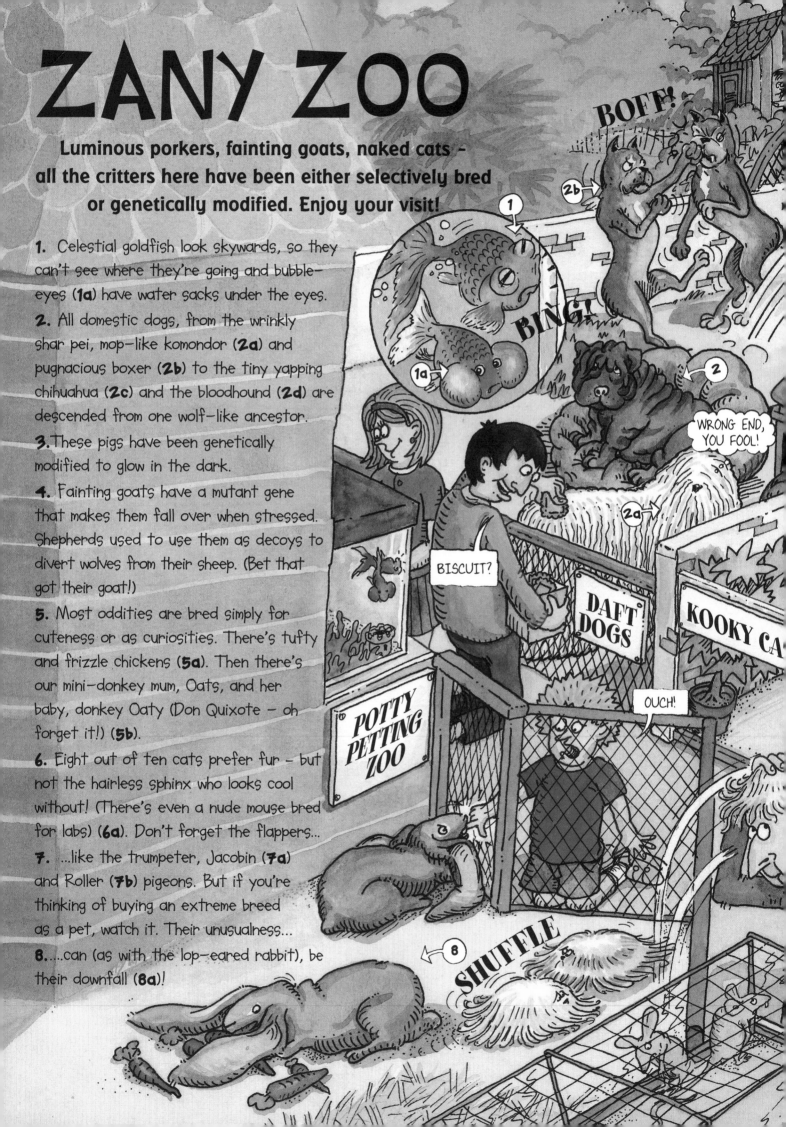

JUMPED-UP GENES...

When people say that noses run in their family, they may mean that they're a snotty bunch (take a close look) or they could be talking about their genes... a subject that should never be sniffed at!

WHY DO I LOOK LIKE THIS, DAD?

I'M NOT SURE, SON. WE'D BETTER READ ON...

Today we call Mendel's particles 'genes'. All the characteristics of all living things are controlled by genes, which are passed on from parents to children. They're like a set of instructions carried inside the cells of your body. Even a tiny simple organism like a bacterium is controlled by over 10,000 genes. It takes around 30,000 genes to form the complete set of instructions for making something as complicated as a human.

Life in jeans, er genes

Mendel's discovery started a whole new science called genetics. And a whole new bunch of scientists, called geneticists (say jen-et-ee-sists). But geneticists couldn't study genes properly until they knew where they were!

PERSONALLY, I PREFER SMART TROUSERS... JEANS PINCH AWFULLY!

By the beginning of the twentieth century, to their surprise, geneticists realised that they'd been staring at them for years... inside the nucleus of a cell.

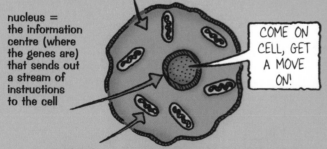

cytoplasm (sigh-toe-plaz-mm) = snot-like slime

nucleus = the information centre (where the genes are) that sends out a stream of instructions to the cell

COME ON CELL, GET A MOVE ON!

mitochondria (my-toe-con-dree-ah) = power stations that break down food and turn it into energy

In truth, you can't actually see a single gene, even with a really powerful microscope. It's far too small. But you can see genes when thousands of them are collected together in one place... on a chromosome.

A chromosome is a worm-like thing which can sometimes be seen inside the nucleus of a cell. They are pretty incredible. Here's why:

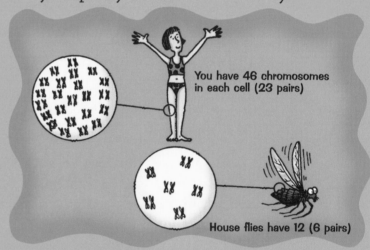

You have 46 chromosomes in each cell (23 pairs)

House flies have 12 (6 pairs)

1 Chromosomes carry all your genes, like a long string of sausages.

2 They spend most of their time hanging around in pairs. Different animals and plants have different numbers of chromosomes.

3 When your skin grows and its cells divide, the chromosomes divide too, so that each new cell carries a full set of instructions that tells it everything it needs to know.

4 A human female egg cell and a male sperm cell carry only 23 chromosomes each. When they join together to make a baby, the two sets make a full set of 46. It's really one of a kind!

IT'S TRUE! THERE'S NOBODY IN THE WORLD QUITE LIKE YOU

THANK GOODNESS!

...And Daft DNA

Okay, so we now know that our genes are the little particles inside our cells that we inherited from our parents and which decide our features – such as being short, tall, red-haired, brown-eyed or big-eared. But let's take a closer look at what they're made of...

DNA FACT FILE

NAME: DNA (deoxyribonucleic acid)
If you want to show off, learn to say it:

> DE-OXY-RYE-BO-NEW-CLAY-IC ACID

THE BASIC FACTS: DNA is the stuff that our chromosomes and genes are made of. Each chromosome is made of a very long, coiled strand of DNA with genes on it.

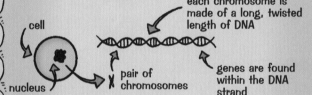

cell

nucleus

pair of chromosomes

each chromosome is made of a long, twisted length of DNA

genes are found within the DNA strand

THE SUFFERING DETAILS: DNA contains four kinds of sub-unit that scientists call A, C, G and T. The order of these letters along the DNA strand creates the genes, which tell the cells what to become and do. So, DNA is like a secret code for life.

YOU INHERIT GENES FROM YOUR FATHER AND MOTHER

DETECTING DNA

Everyone has a unique DNA code in their cells and today forensic scientists can use bits of DNA in skin and spit left at a crime scene to identify criminals. Across the world, the police are working together to set up a database of criminals' DNA to be checked if any DNA is found at a crime scene.

GOTCHA!

GETTING DIRECTIONS

In 1988, scientists set about mapping every one of the 30,000 genes that make up a human.

WHAT IS IT?

A MAP OF YOU!

By 2005 they had found the areas of DNA linked to over 1500 diseases caused by the faulty copying of genes within the cells of the body. One such disease is cystic fibrosis (sis-tic fi-bro-sis) which attacks the lungs and can be fatal.

Bet you never knew!

1 At the end of the 1990s scientists developed a spray to help fight cystic fibrosis. A patient suffering from the disease breathes in the spray containing healthy genes to replace their damaged genes. The spray helps the genes to travel to the patient's lungs.

2 And it's now possible to test a person's genes to find out whether they are damaged. If they are,

this could cause a deadly disease in the future. Obviously if the disease is one that could be treated, this would be a vital warning, but what if the disease can't be treated? Chances are, the person wouldn't exactly be desperate to hear the horrible news. What would you choose?

I DON'T WANT TO KNOW!

FAIRGROUND FRIGHTENERS

The whirling, plunging, spinning, twisting rides in the fair will get your heart pounding and give you that stomach-in-the-mouth feeling. So hold onto your dinner...

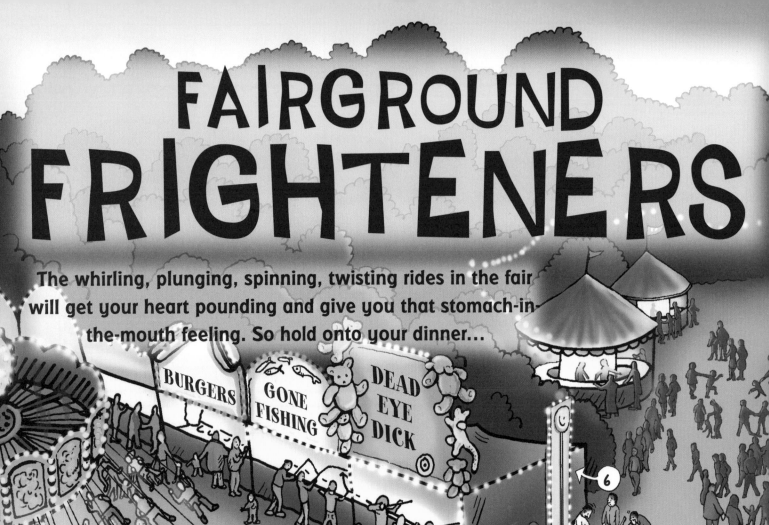

FEEL THE FORCE

1. There's no ride more hair-raisingly terrifying than a rollercoaster. One thing's for sure, as you roar around the loop-the-loop you won't be thinking about gravity, no matter how grave your situation! But rollercoasters work entirely by the force of gravity – there's no motor whatsoever and you are held in tight in your seat by the g-forces.

2. Motorcycle pyramid – this amazing fairground feat can only be done because the weight of each rider is spread out across the whole shape.

3. A fairground freefall ride drops you vertically and for a short while there is nothing to stop you. As you plunge to Earth, falling under gravity, you experience a short period of weightlessness – your stomach might not like it but your mind does. Your body releases adrenaline, which sends you loopy for hours after the ride.

4. A quick spin in the 'cage' is like getting trapped in a tumble-dryer! You get spun around so fast that you get stuck to the outside wall. This effect is called 'centrifugal' (cent-tree-few-gal) force but it's not really a proper force – it's the effect of travelling in a circular path.

5. The 'pirate ship' is really a massive pendulum – the kind of thing that Foucault used to prove that the Earth is spinning.

6. Test your strength – do some work against gravity – DING!

7. Merry-go-rounds spin you round. The faster you go, the higher you fly...

IN THE GRIP OF...
GRAVITY

Gravity is the force which pulls two objects towards each other (not the same forcew your mum uses to make you kiss your ghastly gran, though). It exists all over the universe but is weaker on the Moon and in outer space.

ON A SMALL PLANET IN THE CORNER OF THE MILKY WAY GALAXY IN THE YEAR 1666, LEGEND HAS IT...

Lincolnshire, England

OI! MOVE THE ARROW - IT'S BLOCKING MY VIEW!

...A YOUNG MATHEMATICS SCHOLAR CALLED ISAAC NEWTON WAS SITTING STUDYING BENEATH AN APPLE TREE IN HIS GARDEN. THEN...

CORE, THAT HURT!

BOINK

ISAAAAAAC! YOUR DINNER'S READY!

...AN APPLE LANDED ON YOUNG ISAAC'S HEAD AND PLANTED THE SEED OF AN IDEA IN HIS MIND.

SO, ISAAC FORGOT HIS DINNER AND SET ABOUT WORKING OUT WHAT INVISIBLE FORCE HAD CAUSED THE APPLE TO FALL TO EARTH RATHER THAN FLYING OFF INTO SPACE.

MMM... I MUST STEW THIS OVER

HE CALLED IT 'GRAVITY' AND CONCLUDED THAT IT'S THE SAME FORCE THAT KEEPS OUR FEET ON THE GROUND AND HOLDS THE MOON IN ORBIT IN THE NIGHT SKY.

YIPPEE! I'VE GOT IT!

I THOUGHT THIS GRAVITY STUFF KEPT YOUR FEET ON THE GROUND!

IN 1955, TEST PILOT GEORGE FRANKLIN SMITH FELT THE FULL EFFECTS ON THE HUMAN BODY OF SPEEDING AGAINST GRAVITY, WHEN HE EJECTED FROM A PLANE GOING AT SUPERSONIC SPEED.

ALL WAS GOING WELL FOR GEORGE AS HE BROKE THE SOUND BARRIER IN HIS F-100A SUPER SABRE JET.

MAY THE FORCE BE WITH ME

UNTIL...

...THE JET CONTROLS JAMMED AND THE PLANE WENT INTO A STEEP NOSE-DIVE.

UH, OH... THIS JET-IS-ON ITS WAY DOWN!

SO, GEORGE PULLED THE LEVER TO RELEASE THE EJECTOR SEAT.

BUT AS GEORGE SHOT OUT OF THE COCKPIT, HIS SPEED BOOSTED THE EFFECTS OF GRAVITY AND IT BEGAN TO SQUASH HIS BODY.

GRAVITY IS GETTING ME DOWN!

THE MASSIVE FORCES HAD CAUSED THE FOLLOWING DAMAGE TO GEORGE'S BODY:

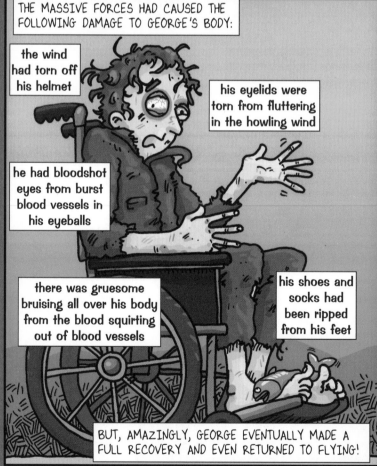

the wind had torn off his helmet

his eyelids were torn from fluttering in the howling wind

he had bloodshot eyes from burst blood vessels in his eyeballs

there was gruesome bruising all over his body from the blood squirting out of blood vessels

his shoes and socks had been ripped from his feet

BUT, AMAZINGLY, GEORGE EVENTUALLY MADE A FULL RECOVERY AND EVEN RETURNED TO FLYING!

NO ONE HAD SURVIVED EJECTION AT SUPERSONIC SPEED BEFORE. BUT WHEN SOME FISHERMEN PULLED GEORGE OUT OF THE SEA WHERE HIS PARACHUTE HAD LANDED, THEY FOUND THAT HE WAS STILL ALIVE...

MMM, SOMETHING'S FISHY HERE!

GIVE 'IM SOME AIR, MEN

...BUT ONLY JUST!

SO, IF YOUR LITTLE BROTHER SAYS, "GRAVITY... WHAT'S IT GOT TO DO WITH ME?" - YOU CAN BRING HIM DOWN TO EARTH WITH A BUMP AND SAY, "EVERYTHING!"

FABULOUS FREEFALL

curves forwards and your arms and [...] pushed backwards. This makes a la[...] the drag to act upon. So you don't [...] fast. Flying squirrels and sky-divin[...] in mid-air.

1 Try not to look at the ground. Jump out of the plane. Check your parachute is strapped securely to your back. (Actually, do that before you jump!)

2 Start tumbling. That's not something you've got to do – it's something that will happen to you anyway. You'll find your sense of balance can't help you stay upright. You'll feel sick. Try not to panic at this stage.

3 For 15 seconds you fall faster and faster. Every second you fall 9.8 metres faster until you hit 50 metres a second (160–240km/h). That's the maximum speed you can fall. It's called terminal velocity. Gulp!

4 Good news. You won't fall any faster because the air slows you down – this force is known as drag.

5 Here's your chance to practise your freefall parachuting technique. Try to fall face downwards. Spread your arms and legs and stick your stomach out. You'll find your body

6 One minute later. Had fun? Good. You've got 1250 metres to go and you're going to hit the ground in 25 seconds. Better pull your parachute rip chord now or you'll really fall foul of gravity. And make a rather deep hole!

7 As you land, make sure you drop down to a squatting position. Bending your knees soaks up some force as you hit the ground. Enjoyed it? Great – you'll be falling over yourself to make another jump.

Bet you never knew!

If you don't happen to have a parachute, things can get a teensy bit more difficult. In 1944 Flight–Sergeant Nicholas Alkemade was in desperate danger 5500 metres above Germany. His plane was on fire and his parachute was burnt to a cinder. He jumped and fully expected to die. But he was lucky. He fell on top of a tree and then onto a deep bank of snow, and as a result, much of the force of his fall was soaked up. Alkemade survived to tell his remarkable story and he didn't even break any bones!

GO BATTY WITH GRAVITY

Amaze your friends with a bat that balances by its nose and 'magically' defies gravity.

You will need:

- 2 sheets of white A4 paper
- 2 small coins (such as pennies)
- a cocktail stick (blunt both ends)
- paper glue
- a pencil, colouring pens or paint

1 Trace this half-bat onto one half of your sheet of paper, fold it on the dotted line and cut it out. Or, enlarge this bat by 300% using a photocopier and cut it out.

2 Fill in the bat's features and colour or paint it – grey or black is scarier, but multicoloured will get your bat noticed by others.

3 Now tape the two identical coins underneath the front wing-tips of your bat. Be careful to position them in exactly the same place on each wing.

4 Take the blunt-tipped cocktail and stick it exactly in the centre of the underside of your bat, with the point sticking out by 1cm from the top of its head.

5 Now hide the coins and cocktail stick by gluing the other piece of white paper to your bat. Carefully cut around the edges. Finish drawing and decorating your bats' features.

6 Perch your bat on the end of your finger or a shelf corner and watch it defy gravity! (Only you know the smashing secret of the brilliant balancing ballast.)

Amazin' anti-gravity arms

Make your arms defy gravity (don't worry... it's 'armless).

1 Stand with your arms by your sides and your hands pressed against your thighs. Now ask your friend to hold your arms in this position as you try to bring your arms up.

2 Count to 60, then ask your friend to let go of your arms. Relax and feel your arms floating upwards as your muscles continue working.

Nasty Newton

Newton may have been a genius, but he was also a grumpy guts. See if you can guess which of these Newton nasties are true and which are false.

1. When Newton was three, his mum re-married. Isaac hated his stepdad so much that he killed him.
TRUE/FALSE

2. As a child, Newton's favourite toy was a model windmill powered by a mouse in a wheel.
TRUE/FALSE

3. At school, Newton had no friends until he thumped the school bully, then he became popular. Isaac was smaller than his opponent, but used his cunning to help him win the fight.
TRUE/FALSE

4. Newton's dog knocked over a candle and 20 years hard work went up in flames. So Newton drew his sword and killed the dog.
TRUE/FALSE

5. When Newton became a professor of mathematics at Cambridge, no one attended his bum-numbingly boring lectures, but he carried on talking to an empty room.
TRUE/FALSE

BLACK HOLE!

It's the ultimate in gravitational pull - the super-hungry big black hole! How does it form? What does it do? You too will get sucked in if you get too close!

DEATH STAR

1. All stars like our Sun begin life as a nebula (**1a**), then become a protostar (**1b**) before forming fully (**1c**) for a few billion years. Eventually stars run out of fuel when there's no more hydrogen to burn into helium. The core shrinks until hot enough for the helium to form into carbon. The outer layers swell up to have a cooler redder surface, and then form into a red supergiant (**1d**). If it's big enough, the star will explode into a giant supernova (**1e**) then turn into a supercompressed, very dense black hole (**1f**).

2. The black hole's gravitational pull is so great that nothing escapes it... not even light (**2a**)! No other object has greater gravity or suction power (**2b**).

3. You can tell a black hole from a distance because its companion star is circling with a large, fast orbit and gases are sucked into the black hole. Scientists think there's a black hole in the middle of the Milky Way.

4. Approaching the black hole, all matter is mashed into stellar porridge, where particles are broken down into sub-particles, like a big cement mixer.

5. Around the centre of the hole there is a point beyond which nothing can escape. This is the event horizon, and its centre is the singularity.

6. Entering the hole, all objects, including this unlucky spaceman, experience 'spaghettification', Not a tasty experience!

7. Stars only stand a chance of becoming a black hole if they're at least 30 times bigger than our Sun. If smaller, they shrink to a planetary nebula (**7a**), white dwarf (**7b**), then a dying star (**7c**).

THE GERMINATOR!

Gruesome germs lurked undetected for centuries, and doctors couldn't kill them. But then a 19th-century Frenchman and his long-suffering wife came along with ingenious equipment and some seemingly mad methods. Germs were soon to be terminated!

LOUIS PASTEUR WAS BORN IN DÔLE, FRANCE IN 1822. HE HAD A VERY STRICT CATHOLIC UPBRINGING BY HIS DAD, WHO WAS A TANNER AND ALWAYS MADE HIM WORK HARD.

DAD – I'M FEELING TIRED AND DOLEFUL!

DÔLE

TAN

DO YOUR HOMEWORK OR I'LL TAN YOUR HIDE!

DRIP!

LOUIS DID WORK HARD, AND GAINED MUCH ACADEMIC SUCCESS. IN 1849 HE BECAME A PROFESSOR OF CHEMISTRY AT STRASBOURG UNIVERSITY. THERE HE MET WITH THE RECTOR'S BRIGHT DAUGHTER, MARIE...

BUT LOUIS'S MIND WAS ONLY ON ONE THING...

... WHEN THEY GOT MARRIED, LOUIS TOLD MARIE'S FATHER THAT ALL HE COULD OFFER HER WAS HIS WORK. AND HE WAS RIGHT...

HE HARDLY TALKS TO ME AT ALL!

... BUT MARIE ACTUALLY HELPED LOUIS WITH MANY SCIENTIFIC DISCOVERIES...

... HOW STRUCTURES OF SOME CHEMICALS COME IN TWO FORMS THAT ARE MIRROR IMAGES OF EACH OTHER. THIS LAUNCHED A NEW BRANCH OF SCIENCE USING LIGHT REFLECTED FROM CHEMICALS TO STUDY HOW THE ATOMS IN THEM ARE ARRANGED.

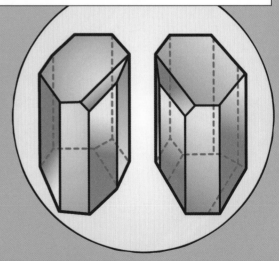

BUT THE PASTEURS' GREATEST WORK WAS ON GERMS. BEFORE LOUIS, DOCTORS BELIEVED THAT DISEASES WERE SIMPLY CAUSED BY BAD SMELLS.

PARDON ME! I'VE GOT SMELLY BUM DISEASE!

FART!

LOUIS FIRST CREATED A SPECIAL FLASK WITH FILTERS TO PREVENT DUST AND AIR GETTING IN, AND BOILED SOME BROTH IN IT. BUT IT WAS A TIME-CONSUMING FLASK, ER TASK.

WHAT'S FOR DINNER TONIGHT?

BOILED BROTH

YUCK! NOT AGAIN

LOUIS FOUND THAT WITH THESE FILTERS, MICRO-ORGANISM GERMS DIDN'T GROW IN THE BROTH. THIS MEANT THEY DIDN'T GET GENERATED SPONTANEOUSLY, BUT CAME FROM THE OUTSIDE – FROM SPORES ON DUST.

AHA! CAUGHT YOU! YOU'RE OUTSIDERS!

DRAT! THE GAME'S UP. HE KNOWS THE SPORE!

LOUIS HAD ALSO DISCOVERED THAT MICRO-ORGANISMS COULD APPEAR IN FERMENTING DRINKS, SUCH AS BEER OR WINE. AT FIRST, NO ONE BELIEVED HIM.

GERMS IN BEER? THAT'S RUBBISSSHHH!

HIC!

SPILL!

MILK ALSO COULD BE CONTAMINATED. BUT PASTEUR AND HIS FRIEND CLAUDE BERNARD WORKED OUT A WAY OF KILLING MILK'S BACTERIA AND MOULDS, AND ALSO SLOWING THE SOURING PROCESS, BY HEATING. HE GAVE THE PROCESS A NAME...

LET'S CALL THIS PROCESS PASTEUR-ISED, AFTER ME!

BOIL!

THOUGHT YOU'D SAY THAT. YOU'RE REALLY MILKING IT!

WINE TOO WAS ALSO HEATED TO KILL ITS BACTERIA.

SOUNDS PURR-FECT TO ME!

LOUIS EVEN DISCOVERED THAT SOME MICRO-ORGANISMS COULD LIVE WITHOUT AIR OR OXYGEN. THIS WAS CALLED ANAEROBIOSIS (AN-AIR-O-BIO-SIS).

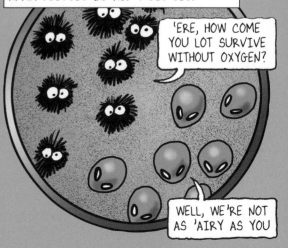

'ERE, HOW COME YOU LOT SURVIVE WITHOUT OXYGEN?

WELL, WE'RE NOT AS 'AIRY AS YOU

LOUIS DISCOVERED THE GERMS THAT CAUSED DISEASES SUCH AS CHICKEN CHOLERA. HIS SOLUTION? HE INFECTED HEALTHY CHICKENS WITH A SMALL AMOUNT OF THE DISEASE BACTERIA!

BUT DESPITE MINOR SYMPTOMS, THE CHICKEN'S IMMUNE SYSTEM KILLED THE WEAKENED CHOLERA BACTERIA, AND MADE THEM RESISTANT TO THE DISEASE. LOUIS HAD HELPED TO DEVELOP VACCINATION (VAX-IN-AY-SHUN).

I FEEL LIGHT AS A FEATHER!

FLAP!

WHAT'S HE DOING? GIVING US CHOLERA?

CLUCK!

TIP! TOE!

I DON'T WANT IT. I'M CHICKEN!

PECK!

YIKES! THEY'RE PECKING ON US!

LOUIS DID THE SAME WITH A VERY DANGEROUS DISEASE CALLED ANTHRAX, WHICH ATTACKED CATTLE. HE HAD FIRST WEAKENED THE ANTHRAX BACTERIA BY EXPOSING THEM TO CERTAIN CHEMICALS.

HISS!

OXYGEN

YIKES! THE CHOKE'S ON US!

IN 1885 LOUIS SAVED THE LIFE OF A BOY CALLED JOSEPH MEISTER BY INJECTING HIM WITH A VACCINE AGAINST THE KILLER DISEASE RABIES. THE BOY HAD BEEN BITTEN BY A RABIES-RIDDEN DOG.

FEELING BETTER SON?

GRR!

DROOL!

I'M GETTING BETTER QUITE RABIDLY

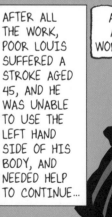

AFTER ALL THE WORK, POOR LOUIS SUFFERED A STROKE AGED 45, AND HE WAS UNABLE TO USE THE LEFT HAND SIDE OF HIS BODY, AND NEEDED HELP TO CONTINUE...

ARE YOU ABLE TO WORK LOUIS?

YES, BUT I'VE GOT NO ENERGY LEFT!

DON'T WORRY, THERE'S PLENTY MORE 'LEFT' TO READ ON GERMS ON THE NEXT PAGE...

Foul Germ Facts

Fowl Fungus

Substances that help protect the body from germ attack, called antibiotics, have been found in some moulds such as penicillium (pen-e-silly-um). One such antibiotic was discovered by American scientist Selman Waksman (1888-1973). Glory-hunting Selman was so keen he tested over 10,000 (yes, you did read that right, ten thousand) suitable fungi. Phew!

He found what he was looking for in the throat of a sick hen! He was extremely egg-sited...

It was a fungus, called streptomyces (strep-toe-my-sees), that killed other germs even whilst it was making the fowl feel foul. Waksman discovered more fungi by grovelling in the hen coop amongst the smelly droppings – but it was worth it, because in 1952 he won the Nobel Prize. Streptomyces proved good for bumping off the bacteria that cause plague.

Stomach Rot

In 1982 Australian scientist Barry Marshall became convinced that the painful ulcers some people get in their stomachs were caused by bacteria. It was a gut instinct all right – but certain germs always seemed to be in the victims' stomachs. Barry decided on a revolting experiment, but help wasn't at hand...

I'M LOOKING FOR VOLUNTEERS

SORRY, I HAVEN'T GOT THE GUTS

Instead, he drank the disgusting bacteria and stuck a special viewing tube, called an endoscope, into his own stomach to check what they were up to. Barry indeed found that the gruesome germs were busy making ulcers.

Swollen and Spotty

Viruses are responsible for two really rather wacky diseases that you might come across in childhood.

If your face has swollen up and is really painful, and you feel sick, you may be suffering from the viral disease mumps. This virus infects the spit-making glands on the sides of your face. The disease gets better on its own, so the best treatment is to go to bed, take painkillers and keep the area warm. Until then you've just got to face it!

swollen glands

If you're feeling sick and achy and feverish and your back and chest and forehead are covered in itching watery

don't pick them!

pus-filled spots, you probably have chickenpox. And you don't need to go near chickens to pick it up! The best treatment is to rest and wait for the spots to become scabs and dry out. And don't pick them or they'll leave little round scars. At least you won't get chickenpox again because your body will be immune to the virus!

Germflakes

Every day you shed 10 billion flakes of dead skin – they just drop off your body as fresh skin forms underneath. You can see a few of these bits if you turn a dirty pair of black trousers inside-out. At least two-thirds of these bits carry bacteria and viruses.

So when you clean your room you stir up these bits and

breathe in your own skin and germs!

SICKLY SCHOOL BUS

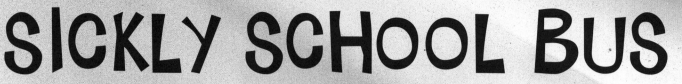

Bacteria and viruses are everywhere, especially on a sniffy, snotty school bus on a winter's morning! Get a uniquely yucky look at these gruesome germs, but do your best to avoid them!

1. With lots of coughing and sneezing, it's no wonder the cold virus is spreading! A virus is a microscopic particle that can only reproduce in other living cells. But how?

2. Carried by dirty fingers or sneezed droplets, first the virus extends a receptor (**2a**) into the cells of your nose (**2b**) and invades it (**2c**). Once inside the cell (**2d**) it starts an 8–12–hour–long process for symptoms to show. Causing an infection to attack the cell's nucleus (**2e**), it uses the cell to reproduce (**2f**), and as the cell dies, it spreads (**2g**) through the nasal cavity. It's quick, efficient and vicious!

3. Take a look at the flu virus! It causes cold, fever and shivering (**3a**). This fluey fellow should be in bed!

4. The marauding mumps virus (**4a**) gives you lumps and swelling around the neck and throat.

5. The chickenpox virus is another a strange looking agent. It causes red spots that are very itchy (**5a**).

6. The measles virus also spreads easily. It can make you feel ghastly, giving you even bigger red skin sores (**6a**).

7. Bacteria are one–celled micro–organisms which live inside and all around us. It even has a tail–like flagellum (**7a**) which helps to propel it around!

8. Bacteria reproduce very rapidly, the most common are the round clustering coccus (**8a**), the rod–shaped clinging bacillus (**8b**) and the corkscrew–shaped bouncing spirillum (**8c**).

9. Bacteria are in sour milk, unbrushed teeth and bad breath (**9a**), mouldy sandwiches (**9b**), smears of snot on the window (**9c**), dog poo (**9d**), and saliva–soaked pea–shooters (**9e**).

10. Protists are another kind of germ, here hidden under fingernails. Yuck!

11. But fresh yoghurt has healthy bacteria!

12. To help avoid the nasty germs, eat lots of fruit – especially oranges to get vitamin C, and zinc–rich bananas.

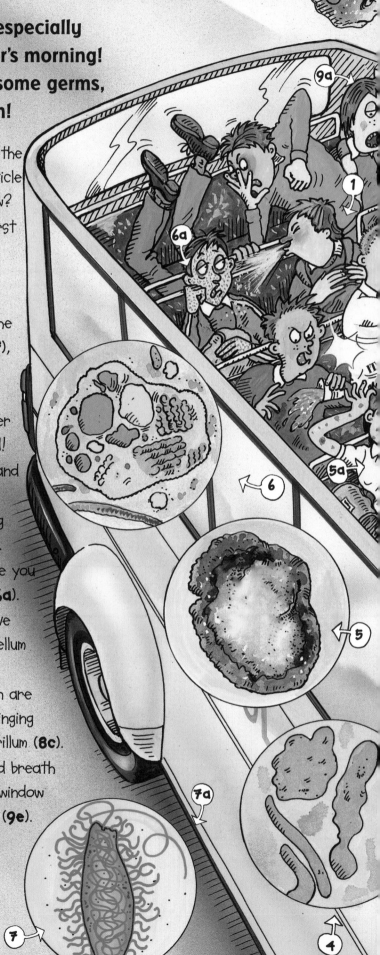

SOAPY SOLUTION: FIGHTING GRIME

There are millions of germs and other microbes on your hands right now. Some are harmless, but others may cause ghastly diseases. Let's see how easy – or difficult – it is to wash them off and prevent the spread of infection.

You will need:
- cooking oil
- ground spice
- cold tap water
- warm tap water
- hand soap
- a hand towel
- a sink or basin

WARNING! Cooking oil mixed with spice is messy. Try not to spill any on the floor or furniture. Wear old clothes and do this experiment over a sink or draining board. Ask an adult to help.

SMEAR

OOZE

1 You can't see germs, such as bacteria, so begin by finding some pretend germs – a little ground mixed spice powder will do the trick and looks suitably brown and yucky. Carefully pour a little cooking oil into your cupped hand and then wipe your hands together to spread the oil all over them.

AACHOO!

SPRINKLE

2 Sprinkle some spice powder on to your oily hands so they're covered in the fake germs. Rub your hands together to spread the yuck evenly.

SPLASH!

RUB

3 Wash your hands under a cold water tap. Rub them together under the flowing water. It's difficult to wash this way, isn't it? See how many 'germs' remain on your fingers and under your nails!

4 Add more oil and spice 'germs' to your hands and try this time to wash them under warm tap water. This should be a little better, but the germs still won't go away.

RUB

5 Repeat step 4 but use some hand soap with the warm water. See how much easier this makes it to clean off the germs. Time how long it takes to get rid of them, even those under your nails and between your fingers. Next time you wash your hands, remember how thorough you should be.

FOAM

6 Okay, so you've now washed your hands clean, but where have the germs gone? Hopefully, most of them are down the drain and out of harm's way. But look around where you've been doing your experiment. What do you see?

7 Check out the sink itself. Are there oily, scummy stains all around it, covered in spice 'germs'. Maybe you didn't do much of a job of cleaning it after you'd washed your hands? Better own up to an adult and ask them to reach for some detergent!

8 Then there's the tea-t... sink cloth, draining b... worktop, taps, floor... How many places did you wipe those 'germs' before you got round to washing them off your hands. You see now why it's so important to keep yourself and your home clean and fresh.

How does speaking spread flu?

Germs aren't just spread on grubby hands... coughing and sneezing will also infect others around you. Even speaking can be hazardous...

1 When you've got a nice mouthful of spit, press your nose against the mirror. Now say the word 'SPIT' loudly.

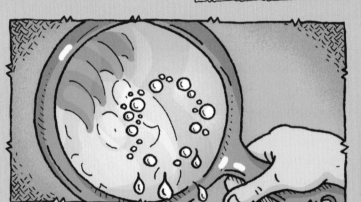

2 Look closely at the mirror and see just how many spit droplets have covered it. Terrifying! Now wipe the mirror clean with soapy water.

3 Repeat step 1 but this time say the word 'DRY' loudly. There should be fewer droplets of spit on the mirror. Letters such as 'P' and 'T' in 'SPIT' actually spray spit. And these droplets could be hiding millions of flu viruses. Again, wipe the mirror clean.

4 Next time you're feeling under the weather, don't cough or sneeze in someone else's face, or talk loudly at them.

55

SICKENING SORES

Cold sores are disgusting scabs that appear on lips and noses. They're not caused by colds, but by a horrible little virus - called Herpes simplex - that likes to lurk inside people's faces.

1. The Herpes simplex virus is a sneaky germ. Once it infects the skin, it reproduces in a cell, then creeps up a nerve strand... and hides out in the nerve's nucleus (1a). A nice warm safe place for a virus to hang out! (By the way, in real life the virus is impossible to see with the naked eye.)

2. They don't do anything here except hang out... until the victim is run down, ill with a cold or flu or had too much exposure from sunlight... and then they get active. They're self-duplicating, scab-making, mean machines! When a person's defences are low, they get going...

3. ...slipping and zipping all the way down a nerve as if it was a secret slide (3a)!

4. Their destination - the outer layer of the lip, called the epithelium. They jump from the nerve to the skin cells (4a). This is where the going gets really nasty and the virus does its damage.

5. The virus latches on to an epithelium cell, using a kind of chemical hook or anchor called a 'receptor' molecule.

6. Once inside the cell, the virus is very sneaky. It loses its outer spiky coating to climb inside the cell's nucleus and unleash its nasty little genes...

7. ...so they can hijack the nucleus of the cells...

8. ...and make it reproduce their genes! Result — more horrid Herpes simplex. The new viruses pop their spiky coats back on.

9. The infected epithelium cells go bananas. Vilely invaded by the virus, they form bubbles on the skin. These are called vesicles, and better known as cold sores. The vesicles swell, burst and weep, forming sickening scabs.

10. The fluid that weeps from a cold sore is infectious. The viruses in it just trying to get passed on to the next person. The bad news is that once you get a cold sore, you have the virus in your body for the rest of your life. The good news is that each outbreak only lasts a few weeks and creams and pills can control them fairly successfully. So if you ever have one, no sickening snogging (yuck), and if you touch a cold sore, wash your hands thoroughly straight afterwards!

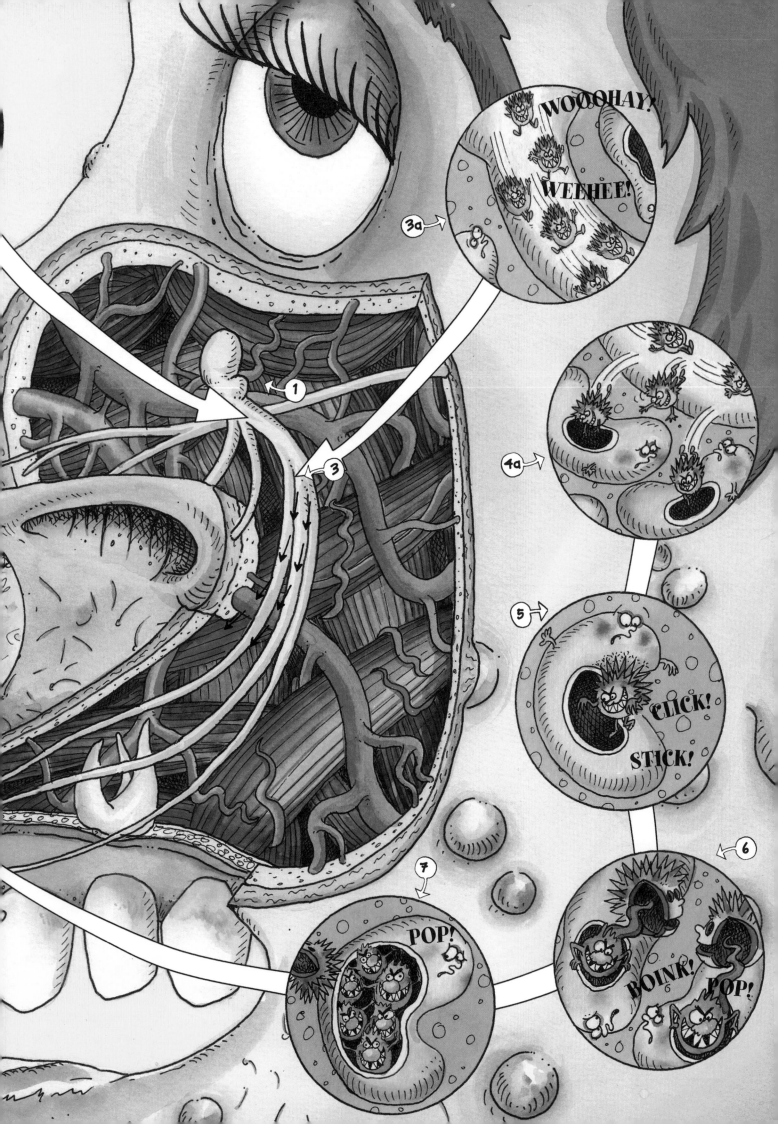

BEASTLY BACTERIA

Beastly bacteria cause diseases such as the plague and the lung disease tuberculosis. They're all tiny and can be found in all different shapes... and millions would fit in a matchbox.

COUGH!

Imagine everything became invisible and the microbes currently invisible began to glow. Everything – trees, houses, people, school dinner and dogs' poo would disappear. But you could see where they were because the outlines of these objects and everything else would be picked out in glowing microbes. Yes, everything is crawling with the little monsters! Let's go to a class on one microbe group – bacteria...

HORRIBLE SCIENCE QUESTION TIME
TOP SCIENTIST PROFESSOR VERA TEENY ANSWERS YOUR QUESTIONS ON BACTERIA

WHAT IS A BACTERIA?

It's a bacterium, actually. If you have two or more then they're called bacteria.

HUH – DON'T GET SNOTTY WITH US! OK, THEN, WHAT ARE BACTERIA?

Any one of thousands of types of tiny living things. They have roughly the same features.

three outer layers of slime to protect body from drying out

nucleus area contains DNA

To get around, bacteria wriggle through the water in which they live. Some beat a whip-like tail called a flagellum (fla-gell-um) and others have tiny beating hairs called cilia (silly-a).

WRIGGLE!

BEAT!

SO HOW MANY TYPES OF BACTERIA ARE THERE?

Lots

CAN YOU BE MORE EXACT?

No

Scientists in Southern California found 61 types of bacteria in a hot spring in Yellowstone National Park and 57 were unknown. Some boffins think every pinch of soil could contain 10,000 different types of bacteria but they haven't got round to counting them all yet.

Any volunteers to count them?

An average-sized lawn holds countless billions of individual bacteria – about 4.5kg by weight. And they're eaten by an army of tiny protists and slimy nematode worms with no eyes and six rubbery lips.

WHERE ELSE DO BACTERIA LIVE?

Where don't they live! Most are in 'cities' of slime in massive piles like tower blocks 200 micrometres high. (That's big by their standards.) Favourite places are sewage pipes, false teeth, contact lenses, the guts and just about everywhere else you can image...

SO WHAT DO BACTERIA DO ALL DAY?

Well, they eat and divide to make new bacteria and they eat and they divide and when they're bored with that they divide and eat. Well, I suppose they could play football under the microscope but then they might be caught off-slide! Ha, ha – sorry, just my little joke.

MUNCH! SPLIT!
MUNCH! MUNCH!
SPLIT! SPLIT!

PUZZLES

Doctor, Doctor?

A patient has a boil on his nose. The boil is caused by bacteria and the red swelling is full of lovely golden pus. Oh well, it could be worse — it could be a boil on the foot.

Then you'd have pus in boots! Anyway, what forms this substance?
a) It's gas given out by the bacteria.
b) It's blood sucked in by the bacteria.
c) It's a mixture of dead blood cells and dead bacteria.

> **HORRIBLE HEALTH WARNING!**
> DON'T squeeze the boil. This allows more germs into the body and you may squirt pus in your eyeball. Yuck!

What's Snot Right?

A nutty research student said he was taking a peek down this microscope at some nasty nasal ooze when he discovered a new virus that might be giving people a flu-like disease.

WE USED TO LIVE IN A LOVELY WARM NOSE...

... BUT A STUDENT 'PICKED' US FOR HIS RESEARCH

But his professor told him he should 'nose' better than to think he'd found a virus like this. What was wrong with the student's claim?

Teacher's Tea-break Teaser

Arm yourself with this treacherously tricky teaser and a pencil and terrorize your teacher's tea-break. Beat out a little tune on the staffroom door. When it opens, smile an angelic smile and ask:

I WAS WONDERING IF BACTERIA WOULD EAT THIS PENCIL?

I WISH THEY'D EAT YOU!

If your teacher knows the correct answer, you'll eventually hear the reply, "Neither yes or no, but half of it." Bacteria will happily eat the wooden bit but the 'lead' is actually baked clay and graphite (a form of pure carbon). Bacteria can't eat this and that's the reason why bacteria don't eat diamonds either because they're made of pure carbon, too.

Bubble Trouble

Soap will make bubbles on your hands as layers of soap and water trap air. Oh, so you've noticed! Well, take a good look at the surface of the bubble. At just 50 micrometres thick, it's thinner than a stick insect on a diet. It's actually one of the tiniest things you can see without a microscope.

But air bubbles aren't the only things in soap suds. Which of these WON'T be found in any kind of soap?

air bubbles

special germ-eating mites

smelly fat from a dead pig

NICE PONG

perfume so you don't smell the fat

friendly viruses that cause bacteria to mutate

titanium dioxide chemical

59

PUZZLE ANSWERS

Are you a brilliant boffin or brain-dead buffoon? Find out how you rated with the Horrible Science Annual's beastly, boggling brainteasers...

Crazy Camouflage (p17)
Pattern 3

Rep-tiles (p17)
1. Venomous (the series has 3-, 4-, 5-, 6-, 7- and 8- letter words)
2. Slither (the series has words in alphabetical order, starting N, O, P, Q, R, S)
3. Ugly (every word starts with a vowel, A, E, I, O or U)

Spot the Difference (p17)

Lazy Lizard Race (p17)
When the two lizards meet, obviously they are both the SAME distance from the finish, which is 20 metres away.

Savage Space-farers (p27)
1. Fruit flies were the first animals in space.
2. Laika is a national hero in Russia.
3. Able and Baker were the first monkeys to survive space flight.

60

4. The Tilapia was the first fish in space.
5. The cat went too. (Maybe they couldn't find a cat sitter.)
6. Worms from an experiment onboard the Space Shuttle **Columbia** were found still alive in the wreckage after the disaster.
7. Pigs in space? Er, no! But...
8. Guinea pigs – yes – (and rats too).
9. Donkeys – no. (they like a stable environment.)
10. Mice and rats have both been, as have crickets, bees, spiders, tortoises, wasps, beetles, frogs, newts, snails and ants.

Stars In Their Eyes (p27)

A Spationaut – France (European)
B Cosmonaut – Russia
C Astronaut – US (and UK)
D Tailonaut – China
Argonaut might sound like the name for an Argentinian astronaut (and Argentina do have their own space program) but argonaut is actually the name for a sailor on the Greek ship Argo.

Nasty Newton (p59)

1. FALSE Apparently, Newton did hate his stepdad, but only thought about killing him!
2. TRUE; 3. TRUE; 4. FALSE He wasn't quite that mean. He just rewrote the work from memory;
5. TRUE

What's Snot Right? (p59)

As every germ research student should know, all viruses are much too small to be able to see under an ordinary optical microscope like this one. You'd need a very powerful type of microscope called an electron microscope to view them.

Doctor , Doctor? (p59)

c) The blood cells died heroically fighting the bacteria.

Bubble Trouble (p59)

Soap manufacturers don't put germ-eating mites or friendly viruses in their products.

PICTURE CREDITS

6–7 Robin Carter; 8–10 Geri Ford; 11 Chantal Kees; 12–13 Patrice Aggs; 14–15 Faz Choudhury; 16 Peter Kavanagh; 17 Gary Northfield; 18–19 Yann LeGoec; 20–22 Geri Ford; 23 Paul Peart Smith; 24–25 Tom Connell; 26 Gemma Hastilow; 27 Faz Choudhury; 28–29 Tom Connell; 30–32 Dave Smith; 33 Tony de Saulles; 34–35 Yann LeGoec; 36–37 Tony de Saulles; 38–39 Dave Evans; 40–42 Dave Smith; 43 Tony de Saulles; 44 Gemma Hastilow; 45 Tony de Saulles; 46–47 Yann LeGoec; 48–50 Kev Hopgood; 51–53 Robin Carter; 54–55 Gemma Hastilow; 56–57 Yann LeGoec; 58–61 Tony de Saulles